# When Business Kills

# When Business Kills

*The Emerging Crime of Corporate Manslaughter*

Sarah Field
Lucy Jones

BEP BUSINESS EXPERT PRESS

First published in 2018 by
Business Expert Press, LLC
222 East 46th Street, New York, NY 10017
www.businessexpertpress.com

ISBN-13: 978-1-63157-964-6 (paperback)
ISBN-13: 978-1-63157-965-3 (e-book)

Business Expert Press Business Law Collection

Collection ISSN: 2333-6722 (print)
Collection ISSN: 2333-6730 (electronic)

Cover and interior design by S4Carlisle Publishing Services
Private Ltd., Chennai, India

First edition: 2018

10 9 8 7 6 5 4 3 2 1

Printed in the United States of America.

# Abstract

This book aims to explain in clear, accessible language the approach taken by government to corporate offending resulting in a fatality in both the United Kingdom and the United States. The key provisions of the statutory offence of corporate manslaughter, introduced into the United Kingdom in 2008, are examined, and set in context through a consideration of their relationship with prosecution for fatalities at work via the Health and Safety at Work etc Act 1974. Further contextualization is made through comparison with the current position in the United States, highlighting both similarities and differences in approach to occupational fatalities. The range of potential penalties is discussed with particular focus on the sentencing guidelines that apply after February 2016. Concluded corporate homicide cases are reviewed in order to assess the current regime in terms of financial penalties and to shine light on the evolving approach of the prosecuting authorities and the courts to these offenses.

# Keywords

business, companies, corporate homicide, corporate manslaughter, health & safety, penalties

# Contents

# Acknowledgment

Thanks to the team at Business Expert Press/Momentum Press for their support in the preparation of this book and thanks to the University of Brighton for providing a stimulating environment that fosters both teaching and research excellence.

# CHAPTER 1

# The Common Law Framework

Prior to the enactment of the Corporate Manslaughter and Corporate Homicide Act (CMCHA) 2007,[1] the offense of corporate manslaughter in the United Kingdom relied upon the common law. The common law background is important because it highlights how corporate criminal liability has been plagued by the issue of how a corporation becomes criminally liable, and also because the existing common law offense of gross negligence manslaughter continues to apply to individuals, even after the enactment of CMCHA.

In common with the position under U.S. law, criminal liability in the United Kingdom typically requires the establishment of a prohibited act or conduct, together with an accompanying, and concurrent, mental attitude encapsulated in the Latin phrase, *actus non facit reum nisi mens sit rea.*[2]

The first requirement is the commission of an act forbidden by law, the *actus reus,* that leads to – causes – the final consequence. Historically, this has generally referred to the positive commission of an act, and there has traditionally been resistance to the imposition of criminal liability for failure to act. Nonetheless, the criminal law does recognize that this

---

[1] The offense is called corporate manslaughter in England, Wales, and North Ireland and corporate homicide in Scotland.

[2] Per Lord Hailsham in *Haughton v. Smith* [1975] AC 476 at pp.491-492, "Properly translated, this means 'An act does not make a man guilty of a crime, unless his mind be also guilty.'"

may occur, albeit exceptionally.[3] These exceptions have been restricted to cases where a duty has been imposed by statute, or has arisen because of contractual or public duties, or where the accused has inadvertently created a danger which he is then required to take steps to avert, or where the law deems him to owe a duty of care to the victim.

## Manslaughter Under the Common Law

Where the prosecution are seeking a conviction for manslaughter, they will first need to prove that the defendant committed the *actus reus* of that offense, namely the unlawful killing of a human being.

English common law distinguishes two principal forms of involuntary manslaughter: unlawful act (constructive) manslaughter and killing by gross negligence. Criminal liability for the former involves an act which is unlawful in itself resulting in death, while liability for the latter arises where the victim is owed a duty of care by the perpetrator, and while the defendant's conduct is lawful in itself, it is carried out in such a way that it is regarded as grossly negligent and therefore a crime. The former essentially involves the construction of a greater crime out of a lesser crime where death results from the intentional commission of a criminally unlawful and dangerous act, whereas liability for the latter relies on the defendant owing a duty of care to the victim and the gravity of the breach of that duty. Until 2007, where an individual was killed as a result of corporate negligence, a prosecution would normally be based on the common law offense of gross negligence manslaughter.

In addition to establishing the *actus reus*, the prosecution must also prove that the defendant committed the *actus reus* while in a certain state of mind i.e., on proof of fault, traditionally known as *mens rea* or a "guilty mind." There are three principal states of mind which separately or together can constitute the necessary *mens rea* for a criminal offense: intention, recklessness, and negligence. Negligence consists of falling

---

[3]"Unless a statute specifically so provides, or . . . the common law imposes a duty upon a person to act in a particular way towards another . . . a mere omission to act [cannot lead to criminal liability]." (per Lord Diplock, *R v. Miller* [1983] 1 All ER 978.)

below the standard of the ordinary reasonable person. The test is objective, based on the hypothetical person, and involves the defendant either doing something the reasonable person would not do, or not doing something which the reasonable person would do.

In the case of gross negligence manslaughter, the negligence standard is higher than for other offenses with a negligence requirement: in order for a defendant to incur criminal liability for manslaughter, the culpability element requires the negligence to be *gross*. In *R v. Bateman*,[4] where a doctor's patient had died during labor, Lord Hewart CJ explained this concept thus:

> "[I]n order to establish criminal liability the facts must be such that, in the opinion of the jury, the negligence of the accused went beyond a mere matter of compensation between subjects and showed such disregard for the life and safety of others as to amount to a crime against the state and conduct deserving of punishment."[5]

Imposing liability on an artificial legal construct such as a company has proved difficult. Legal concepts such as *actus reus, mens rea*, and causation, designed with natural actors in mind, do not easily lend themselves to inanimate entities such as companies.

## Vicarious Liability

The courts have attempted to solve these problems by using a number of techniques to circumvent notions of *actus reus* and *mens rea* so that they could apply to companies. One of these is the doctrine of vicarious

---

[4](1925) 19 Cr App R 8.

[5]In *R v. Adomako* [1994] 3 All ER 79, the leading case on this area of law, an anaesthetist failed to notice the disconnection of the tube from a ventilator supplying oxygen and the House of Lords held that a defendant was properly convicted of involuntary manslaughter if the jury found that the defendant was in breach of a duty of care towards the victim who died, that the breach of duty caused the death of the victim, and that the breach of duty was such as to be characterised as gross negligence and therefore a crime.

liability (or "*respondeat superior*") according to which the *mens rea* and *actus reus* of another are assigned to the defendant. Liability of corporations by way of vicarious liability was initially recognized in *R v. Great North of England Railway Company*[6] and it is now clear that a corporation may be vicariously liable for the negligent acts and omissions of an employee during the course of his employment.[7]

In the U.S. legal system, corporate culpability based on vicarious liability is well established. This exists where the actions or omissions of a company's employees have breached a duty incumbent upon the company. In *New York Central and Hudson River Railroad Company v. United States*,[8] the court determined that a corporation could be imputed with the knowledge of the act and omissions of its employees and that any criminal culpability for those actions – should they be in violation of law – could also be imputed to the corporation. The court's reasoning was that if corporations were permitted prosecutorial immunity for their actions, it would undermine the ability of the government to control and correct any abuses.

In the United Kingdom, subsequent to the failed prosecution of P & O Ferries for the capsize of the Herald of Free Enterprise ferry in Zeebrugge harbor (causing the death of 193 passengers and crew) another alternative approach was mooted; namely whether the deeds (or omissions) and states of mind of two or more employees could be added together, "aggregated," to create vicarious criminal liability in the company which employed them. There is support in the United States for this approach, known as the "collective knowledge" doctrine,[9] according to which companies are vicariously liable for the behavior of their employees, whatever their status in the organization, and by virtue of which, the conduct and fault elements of the employees can be aggregated so as to render the company liable. In other words in the United States, the conduct of one junior employee can be added to that of another to render a company criminally liable.

---

[6](1846) 9 QB 315 (DC).

[7]*Coppen v. Moore (No 2)* [1898] 2 QB 306 (DC).

[8](1909) 212 U.S. 481.

[9]*U.S. v. Time-DC*, 381 F Supp 730 (WD Pa, 1974); and *U.S. v. Bank of New England*, 821 F 2d 844 (1st Circuit).

Different state jurisdictions diverge in their application of state and federal homicide legislation however. In New Jersey, for example, the courts have determined that a company could be committed of involuntary manslaughter, while in New York in *People v. Rochester Railway and Light Co.*,[10] it was held that companies cannot be liable for such crimes, on the grounds that manslaughter requires the killing of one human being by another. The Rochester case proved to have a restrictive influence in terms of the approach to corporate criminal liability until the late 1970s when judicial decisions in a number of states (such as California, Indiana, New York, Pennsylvania, and Texas) started to hold that corporations could in fact incur liability for manslaughter.[11]

In the United Kingdom on the other hand, the courts have ruled that the principle of vicarious liability does *not* extend to the offense of corporate manslaughter.[12]

## The "Identification" or "Directing Mind" Theory

In *R v. HM Coroner for East Kent ex p Spooner* Bingham LJ affirmed that whilst a company may be vicariously liable for the act of its employees, in order for it to be criminally liable for manslaughter: "It is required that the *mens rea* and *actus reus* of manslaughter should be established not against those who acted for or in the name of the company but against those who were to be identified as the embodiment of the company itself."[13]

In other words, in relation to the offense of involuntary manslaughter, a corporation's guilt could only be established under the common law if it was possible to link the grossly negligent act of an employee through a chain of command, to the "controlling" or "directing mind."[14] It was this theory – the "identification" or "directing mind" theory – that formed

---

[10](1909) 195 NY 102.

[11]J. W. Harlow. 2011. "Corporate Criminal Liability for Homicide: A Statutory Framework," *Duke Law Journal* vol. 61/1 p123; C. Wells. 2001. *Corporations, Crime and Accountability*, 2nd ed. Oxford: OUP.

[12](1989) 88 Cr App R 10 (DC).

[13](1989) 88 Cr App R 10 (DC), at p 16.

[14]A. Pinto & M. Evans. 2008. *Corporate Criminal Liability*, London: Sweet & Maxwell p219.

the basis of the common law offense of corporate manslaughter in the United Kingdom. The doctrine established that while individuals in a corporation could face charges of gross negligence manslaughter (or, indeed, unlawful act manslaughter) a corporation would only incur criminal liability for manslaughter through its controlling officers. Criminal liability would exist solely where a person in the organization, who was sufficiently senior to represent the "directing mind" of the company, was proved to have the requisite knowledge and fault required for the offense.

In the United States, in states where there appears to be no legislative intent to make the criminal law apply to corporations, the identification doctrine has also been adopted. This requires that a criminal act be "performed, authorized or tolerated in a reckless manner by a high-ranking managerial agent or member of the board of directors."[15]

The difficulty with this approach in both jurisdictions is identifying the requisite individual in the organization. The complexity of multi-layered structures within a corporation traditionally has proved an obstacle to establishing the necessary link between the culpable conduct of an employee and the "directing mind." Prosecutions, and particularly convictions, in the United Kingdom under this doctrine were so rare that it appeared that the doctrine operated as a barrier to potential corporate criminal liability. The few companies that were successfully convicted of corporate manslaughter prior to 2007 in the United Kingdom were small companies where it was easier to identify a culpable individual within the organization. Similarly, in the United States, this approach has proved much more effective in prosecuting small companies rather than larger corporate entities.[16]

A notable example is *R v. Kite*[17]; the first corporate manslaughter conviction in the United Kingdom. This case concerned OLL Ltd, which was a small company operating an activity center and which was prosecuted following an accident where four pupils drowned on a canoeing trip at the center. Evidence established that the company routinely employed unqualified

---

[15]J. C. Coffee. 1983. "Corporate criminal responsibility," in S. Kadish (ed). *Encyclopaedia of Crime and Justice*, New York: Free Press pp253-264, at p255.

[16]J.C. Coffee. 1999. "Corporate criminal liability: an introduction and comparative survey," in A. Eser et al (eds). *Criminal Responsibility of Legal and Collective Entities*, Berlin: Edition Iuscrim, pp9-38.

[17][1996] 2 Cr. App. R. (S) 295.

staff and did not train them, and that the supervision of the canoeing trip was grossly inadequate. The company was fined £60,000, which was said to represent its entire asset. A conviction was possible in this case because the size of the company meant an individual could be identified as the directing mind.

This has not been the case with large companies. The prosecution of P& O Ferries in 1990 for manslaughter[18] failed principally because there was insufficient evidence to convict individual senior defendants of manslaughter, and therefore *mens rea* could not be attributed to the company. Although there were errors of omission on the part of the Master, Chief Officer, assistant bosun as well as "cardinal faults" by the board of directors, the charge of corporate manslaughter was dismissed by Turner J, who affirmed that it was not possible to identify a single individual as the controlling mind of the company, and who had been grossly negligent.[19]

Parliament has attempted to address the inadequacies of existing provision in the United Kingdom by legislating a specific criminal offense of corporate manslaughter where liability is not limited by the fiction of identification or vicarious liability and where the criminal law can be used as a means of reinforcing the moral values underpinning current regulation.

To this end, in 2007 a new offense of statutory corporate manslaughter was created by The Corporate Manslaughter and Corporate Homicide Act (CMCHA). Reflecting the common law offense of gross negligence manslaughter, the offense only applies where an organization owes a duty of care to a victim arising out of certain specific functions or activities performed by the organization.[20] The CMCHA 2007 is designed to complement the current law; although individuals such as directors and employees cannot be prosecuted individually under CMCHA, they may still face a personal manslaughter charge under the common law.

---

[18]*R v. P & O Ferries (Dover) Ltd* (1990) 93 Cr App R 72.

[19]*R v. P&O Ferries (Dover) Ltd* (1991) 93 Cr App R 72 (Central Criminal Court), per Turner J at p84-85.

[20]CMCHA 2007, s.2.

# CHAPTER 2

# Criminal Legislation

## The Corporate Manslaughter and Corporate Homicide Act 2007

The majority of countries allow corporate bodies to be held accountable for homicide under general criminal law but the United Kingdom is one of the few jurisdictions[1] to have created a specific corporate homicide offense. The Corporate Manslaughter and Corporate Homicide Act (CMCHA) came into force on 6 April 2008[2] (with the exception of the provision relating to liability for death in custodial institutions which was brought into force on September 1 2011).[3] The offense was designed to secure a conviction of an organization, whether small family business, large multinational company or public body, for a criminal offense that properly reflected the seriousness of the worst instances of management failure causing death. The Act is not retrospective and therefore only applies to offenses committed on or after the Act came into force. There are no new duties

---

[1] The Australian Capital Territory is also an exception. It introduced a specific industrial manslaughter offense in the Crimes (Industrial Manslaughter Act) 2003. P. Almond. 2013. *Corporate Manslaughter and Regulatory Reform* (Basingstoke Hampshire: Palgrave Macmillan), pp.35-37.

[2] The Corporate Manslaughter and Corporate Homicide Act 2007 (Commencement No. 1) Order 2008 SI 2008/401.

[3] The Corporate Manslaughter and Corporate Homicide Act 2007 (Commencement No. 3) Order 2011 SI 2011/ 1867. Implementation of the clause covering custody deaths was delayed in order to give police forces and prison services time to inspect their custody facilities and make sure they were up to standard.

or obligations under the Act, and although it is linked to existing health and safety requirements it is not part of health and safety law.

In the United States, although corporations are capable of committing criminal offenses governed by federal law, corporate manslaughter is not a specific criminal offense at this level. The Occupational Safety and Health Act 1970 is the only federal statute on the context of manslaughter but this Act relates to safety and health in the workplace by imposing comprehensive duties on employers as opposed to governing an explicit offense of manslaughter.

The penal codes of individual states may provide organizations be indicted for the offense of homicide by defining the word "person" in the offense to include corporations. For example, the Penal Code of California expressly states that "person" includes a "corporation as well as a natural person."[4] The New York Penal Code states that "a person is guilty of criminally negligent homicide when, with criminal negligence, he causes the death of another person."[5] The homicide section of the Penal Code provides that the victim must be a "human being who has been born and is alive"[6] but does not define the perpetrator. However, in the general definition of terms "person" is stated as meaning "a human being, and where appropriate, a public or private corporation, an unincorporated association, a partnership, a government or a governmental instrumentality."[7] In the case of *People of the State of New York v. Ebasco Services Incorporated*,[8] the court rejected the argument that the reference to human beings in the homicide section meant that a corporation could not commit homicide, and taking note of the Penal Code's general definition of terms confirmed that a corporation could be indicted for corporate homicide.[9]

Alternatively, states may provide for organizations to be liable for manslaughter under the common law. For example, in the State of Michigan, a corporation may be liable for involuntary manslaughter where it can be shown that the victim's death was caused by the defendant's

---

[4]California Penal Code s7.

[5]New York Penal Code s125.10.

[6]New York Penal Code s125.05.

[7]New York Penal Code s10.00 (7).

[8]*People of the State of New York v. Ebasco Services Incorporated* 77 Misc.2d 784 (1974).

[9]The indictment was in fact dismissed on the grounds that there had been a failure to sufficiently particularize the facts constituting the alleged crime.

"gross negligence."[10] The Michelin Penal Code states that unless there is a contrary intention the word "person" includes public and private corporations, co-partnerships, and unincorporated or voluntary associations.[11] However, under the penal codes of individual states, there is no specific offense of corporate manslaughter which relates only to organizations.

## The Offense of Corporate Manslaughter/Corporate Homicide

CMCHA creates an offense which in England, Wales, and Northern Ireland is known as corporate manslaughter and in Scotland as corporate homicide. Organizations to which the Act applies can no longer be convicted of the common law offense of gross negligence manslaughter.[12] The Act provides[13] that a relevant organization may be convicted of corporate manslaughter if the manner in which its activities are managed or organized causes a death and amounts to a gross breach of a duty to take reasonable care for a person's safety. A substantial part of the breach must have been attributable to senior management failure in the organization. The offense only applies where an organization owes a "relevant duty of care"[14] to the deceased person.

The offense is set out in CMCHA Section 1(1):

"An organisation to which this section applies is guilty of an offence if the way in which its activities are managed or organised:

(a) Causes a person's death, and

(b) Amounts to a gross breach of a relevant duty of care owed by the organization to the deceased."

Section 1(3) states: "An organization is guilty of an offence under this section only if the way in which its activities are managed or organized by its senior management is a substantial element in the breach referred to in subsection (1)."

---

[10]G. Forlin.2014. *Corporate Liability: Work Related Deaths and Criminal Prosecutions* (London: Bloomsbury) p.450.

[11]Michigan Penal Code s10.

[12]CMCHA 2007, s20.

[13]CMCHA 2007, s1 (1).

[14]CMCHA 2007, s2.

## What Types of Organizations Are Covered by the Act?

Section 1(2) defines four types of organization, which can commit the offense of corporate manslaughter:

- A corporation
- A department or other body listed in schedule 1
- A police force[15]
- A partnership or trade union or employers' association (if the organization concerned is an employer)

Corporations (incorporated in the United Kingdom or overseas) include public and private companies, limited liability partnerships, and bodies incorporated by statute or Royal Charter such as local authorities and National Health Service bodies. Charitable and voluntary organizations that have been incorporated or operate as partnerships are also potential defendants. CMCHA Schedule 1 lists 48 government departments or other bodies including the Cabinet Office, Home Office, Ministry for Defence, and Crown Prosecution Service. The usual principle that states Crown bodies, such as government departments, cannot be prosecuted does not apply to corporate manslaughter.[16] In addition, the list of organizations to which the offense applies can be extended by secondary legislation.[17] As police forces are not incorporated bodies, CMCHA ensures that police forces are treated as occupiers of premises, and police officers, police cadets etc., are treated as the employees of the police force for which they work.[18] Partnerships (other than limited liability partnerships) do not in English law have legal personality but under the Act they

---

[15]A police force is defined as one within the meaning of (a) (i) the Police Act 1996 (c. 16), or (ii) the Police (Scotland) Act 1967 (c. 77); (b) the Police Service of Northern Ireland; (c) the Police Service of Northern Ireland Reserve; (d) the British Transport Police Force; (e) the Civil Nuclear Constabulary; and (f) the Ministry of Defence Police (CMCHA 2007, s13).

[16]CMCHA 2007, s11.

[17]CMCHA 2007, s21.

[18]It is the Chief Constable of a force who is liable as a corporation sole where there is a prosecution under HSWA 1974.

are treated as corporate bodies and proceedings can be brought against the partnership with fines paid out of partnership funds.

The Act does not apply to individuals and individuals cannot be guilty of aiding, abetting, counselling, or procuring the offense.

## Relevant Duty of Care

The organization must owe a duty of care to the deceased victim under the law of negligence. A duty of care is an obligation of the organization to take reasonable steps to protect a person's safety. CMCHA does not impose new duties of care where these are not currently owed in the law of negligence. Organizations owe duties, not just to their employees, but also to a broad range of others affected by their activities. The duty of care must also be a "relevant duty" under the Act. These are set out in Section 2 and fall into four main categories:

- Employing or controlling workers[19]: This includes an employer's duty to provide a safe system of work for his employees. An organization may also owe duties of care to those whose work it controls or directs even though they are not formally employed by it, such as contractors or volunteers.
- Occupying premises[20]: This covers duties of care in law, both to visitors and non-visitors such as trespassers.
- Supplying goods or services, undertaking construction or maintenance operations or any other activity on a commercial basis: This includes duties owed by manufacturers to ensure the safety of their products, duties owed by National Health Service bodies for medical treatment, duties to ensure adequate safety precautions are taken when repairing a road, or maintaining the safety of vehicles, or carrying on commercial activities such as farming or mining.

---

[19]Between April 2008 and March 2016 in the United Kingdom, there were over 1200 recorded fatalities of workers in the workplace http://www.hse.gov.uk/statistics/, (accessed April 12 2017).

[20]Premises are defined as a tract of land including buildings and movable structures.

- Holding a person in detention or custody[21]: This includes persons detained in a prison, a police station, or in immigration detention facilities; being held or transported under immigration or prison escort arrangements; being placed in premises used to accommodate children and young people on a secure basis; and being detained under mental health legislation.

Whether a duty of care exists is a matter of law for the judge to decide (as opposed to the jury). The "judge must make any findings of fact necessary to decide that question."[22] The judge will then direct the jury as to the existence of the duty of care. It will then be up to the jury to decide if there was a breach of the duty of care and if so how serious that breach was and "how much of a risk of death it posed."[23]

## Causation

The offense of corporate manslaughter requires that the way an organization managed or organized its activities caused the death. The "way" does not have to be unlawful and includes decisions and actions as well as omissions of management. The management failure need not have been the sole cause of death provided it is "a" cause of death, and the "cause of death" was as a result of a gross breach of a relevant duty of care.

## What Is a Gross Breach?

CMCHA states that a breach of a duty of care is a "gross breach" if the conduct in question "falls far below what can reasonably be expected of the organization in the circumstances."[24] This reflects the threshold for the common law offense of gross negligence manslaughter.[25] Whether the breach is "gross" is a question for the jury who must consider whether the

---

[21]This provision was brought into force September 1 2011 by the Corporate Manslaughter and Corporate Homicide Act (Commencement No 3 Order) SI 2011/1867.
[22]CMCHA 2007, s2 (5).
[23]CMCHA 2007, s8 (2).
[24]CMCHA 2007, s1 (4) (b).
[25]R v. Adomako [1994] 3 WLR 288.

organization failed to comply with relevant health and safety legislation and if so, how serious the noncompliance was and how much of a risk of death it posed.[26] In addition, the jury may consider further factors such as the health and safety guidance and how far they were followed, the organization's safety culture and their attitudes, policies, systems, and accepted practices.

## Who Is Senior Management?

For a conviction of corporate manslaughter under CMCHA, there is no need to show a "controlling" or "directing" mind at the top of the company was also personally guilty of manslaughter; however, an analysis of an organization's decision-making processes which led to the death is an important part of the picture. The prosecution must show that the way in which senior management organized or managed the organization's activities was a substantial element in the breach[27] and therefore may aggregate the management failure.[28] The Act defines senior management as persons who play "significant roles" in making decisions about, or in actually managing or organizing, the "whole or a substantial part" of the organization's activities.[29] This clearly includes those in central strategic or operational management roles, or with central responsibility for regulatory compliance, but exactly who else is included will depend upon the nature and scale of the organization's activities. It may include regional managers of national organizations and managers of different operational divisions.[30] The prosecution does not have to prove that the individual senior managers were in breach of duty but only that collectively senior management played a substantial part of the organizations breach.

A parent company will not be liable for the actions of its subsidiaries unless the breach that was the cause of death was sufficiently

---

[26]CMCHA 2007, s8.

[27]CMCHA 2007, s1 (3).

[28]In *R v. Sterecycle (Rotherham) Ltd* (2014) (unreported) the prosecution relied on the aggregate failures throughout the company as opposed to specific acts of individuals. https://www.healthandsafetyatwork.com/corporate-manslaughter/sterecycle-michael-whinfrey, (accessed May 5 2017).

[29]CMCHA 2007, s1(4)(C).

[30]Ministry of Justice. 2007. *Guide to the Corporate Manslaughter and Corporate Homicide Act 2007.* https://www.publications.parliament.uk/pa/cm201516/cmselect/cmdfence/598/598.pdf, , (accessed May 6 2017).

attributable to senior management failures in the parent company. The degree of control and supervision exercised by the parent company over the subsidiary is relevant. In June 2015, CAV Aerospace Ltd, the parent company of CAV Cambridge, was convicted of corporate manslaughter, despite the fact that the incident which led to the fatality occurred within the subsidiary.[31] Charges were brought against the parent company "due to the collective failings in the management and control of CAV Cambridge Ltd," and because all operational decisions regarding the purchasing, delivery, and storage of materials fell within the responsibility of the parent company which had ignored persistent warnings about the dangers of falling stacks of materials in the three years prior to the fatal incident.[32]

## Territorial Extent of the Act

The offense applies if the harm resulting in death is sustained in the United Kingdom or in a set of limited contexts outside the United Kingdom namely, within the United Kingdom's territorial waters (for example an incident involving commercial shipping), on a British ship, aircraft or hovercraft, or on an oil rig or other offshore installation already covered by the U.K. criminal law.[33] It is the injury that caused the death that has to occur within the United Kingdom's jurisdiction rather than the death itself. It is not only British organizations that may be liable under the Act but all relevant organizations operating in the United Kingdom even if incorporated out-side the United Kingdom. Provided the injury that caused the death was within the United Kingdom's jurisdiction, the management failure or breach of the relevant duty can have occurred outside the United Kingdom.

---

[31]The company was also convicted of breach of sections 3(1) and 33(1)(a) of the Health and Safety at Work etc. Act 1974. http://www.cps.gov.uk/news/latest_news/cav_aerospace_ltd_convicted_of_corporate_manslaughter/, (accessed May 3 2017).

[32]The victim died after a stack of metal sheets collapsed on top of him in a warehouse in Cambridge, trapping and crushing him. The metal sheets, which had been delivered to the warehouse at the company's request and for the company's purposes, collapsed as a result of the dangerously high levels of stock in the warehouse. https://www.healthandsafetyatwork.com/corporate-manslaughter/CAV-aerospace-paul-bowers  http://www.tetraconsulting.co.uk/parent-company-convicted-corporate-manslaughter/,(accessed May 3 2017).

[33]CMCHA 2007, s28.

Where a company incorporated outside the United Kingdom, is operating through a locally registered subsidiary, it is likely that the subsidiary, where the fatality occurred, will be the relevant organization to face prosecution for corporate manslaughter as companies within a group structure are separate legal entities. However, this does depend on all the circumstances of each case and a parent company, taking operational decisions for its subsidiary, can be held liable for corporate manslaughter.

## Exclusions from the Act

There are a number of exclusions set out in CMCHA covering deaths connected with certain public and government functions[34]; some of these exemptions are comprehensive and others are partial. Where a comprehensive exemption exists, the Act does not apply in respect of any duty of care that an organization might otherwise owe. Where there is a partial exemption the Act does not apply unless the death relates to the organization's responsibility as an employer (or to those working for the organization) or as an occupier of premises.

Public policy decisions in respect of anything done in the exercise of an exclusively public function and in respect of statutory inspections are excluded, unless the public authority owes the duty in its capacity as an employer or as an occupier of premises. For example, decisions by public bodies or bodies with public functions[35] about the funding of particular health treatments are excluded. Certain activities performed by the armed forces[36] including "peacekeeping operations and operations for dealing with terrorism, civil unrest or serious public disorder, in the course of which members of the armed forces comes under attack or face the threat of attack or violent resistance"[37] are comprehensively excluded. This exemption extends to "related support and preparatory activities and haz-

---

[34]CMCHA 2007, ss3-7.

[35]Public authorities are defined by reference to the Human Rights Act 1998 and include core public bodies such as government departments and local authorities as well as other bodies whose functions are of a public nature. Private companies that carry out public functions are broadly the same position as public bodies.

[36]British Royal Navy, Army and Air Force.

[37]CMCHA 2007, s4 (2).

ardous training."[38] In the light of the number of fatalities of armed forces personnel in noncombat incidents,[39] there have been calls for exemption to be removed in respect of certain training activities.[40] A similar comprehensive exemption is also given to the police and other law enforcement bodies such as immigration authorities, in respect of operations dealing with terrorism and violent disorder and their support and preparatory activities and training.[41]

In addition, there are partial exemptions from the offense other than in respect of the duty of care owed as an employer or occupier, for a range of activities. These include policing and law enforcement activities,[42] emergency services responding to emergencies such as fire and rescue authorities, coastguards, NHS trusts, ambulance services, organ and blood transport services, and the armed forces.[43] Child protection activities and probation services are also covered by partial exemptions.[44]

## Prosecutions under Corporate Manslaughter and Corporate Homicide Act 2007

Prosecutions under CMCHA are complex and usually the incident has occurred a few years before reaching court. For example, in Cotswold

---

[38] CMCHA 2007, s4, s5 (1), s5 (2).

[39] Between 1 January 2000 and 20 February 2016, 135 armed forces personnel died in non-combat incidents, mainly on training exercises. http://www.theguardian.com/uk-news/2016/apr/24/ministry-of-defence-should-lose-crown-immunity-say-mps, (accessed April 25 2017).

[40] U.K. Parliamentary Defence Select Committee. 2016. *Beyond Endurance? Military exercises and the Duty of Care*.HC598. The Report was emphatic that it was wrong for the Ministry of Defence and armed forces to have exemption under the CMCHA where there had been serious findings in hazardous training and section events resulting in a fatality. https://www.publications.parliament.uk/pa/cm201516/cmselect/cmdfence/598/598.pdf, (accessed May 5 2017). The Government Response to the Committee's Report was negative. http://www.parliament.uk/business/committees/committees-a-z/commons-select/defence-committee/defencesubcommittee/inquiries/parliament-2015/inquiry/, (accessed May 5 2017).

[41]CMCHA 2007, s5 (2).

[42]CMCHA 2007, s5 (3).

[43]CMCHA 2007, s6.

[44]CMCHA 2007, s7.

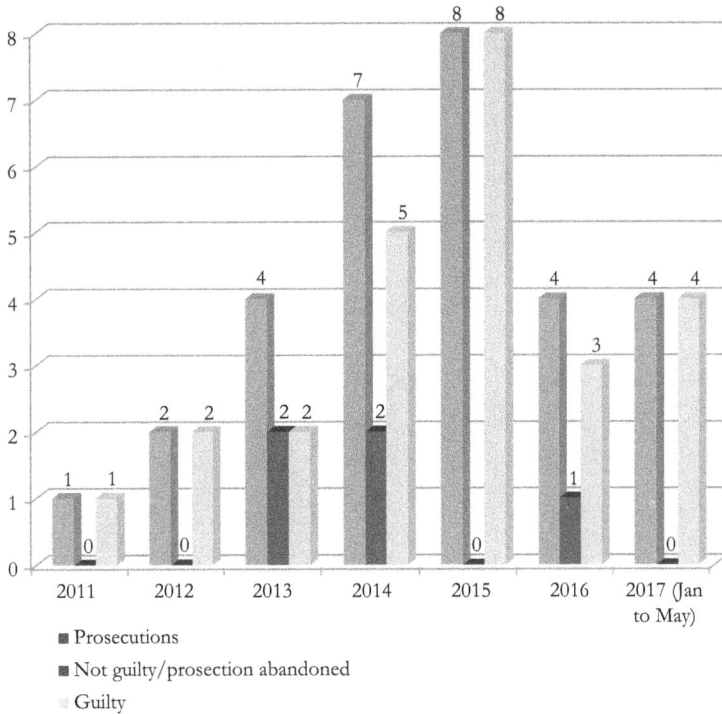

**Chart 2.1 Prosecution outcomes for corporate manslaughter under CMCHA (England, Wales and Northern Ireland)**

Geotechnical Holdings Ltd, the accident occurred in 2008 and conviction secured in 2011, and in Cheshire Gates and Automation Ltd, the accident occurred in 2010 and conviction was secured in 2015.

Since the coming into force of the CHCMA on 6 April 2008, there have been 30 prosecutions and 25 convictions under the CMCHA. Although this represents a small proportion of the number of prosecutions brought as a result of fatalities at work,[45] (where the majority of prosecutions are for breaches under HSWA) the number of successful prosecutions against companies for manslaughter is significantly greater than under the previous common law regime.

---

[45]http://www.hse.gov.uk/prosecutions/, (accessed May 9 2017.).

# CHAPTER 3

# Using Health and Safety Legislation for Corporate Killing

An alternative or an additional course of action, where there has been fatality caused by corporate act or omission, is to use health and safety legislation. Although there are overlaps between corporate manslaughter and health and safety offences resulting in death, the offences are different and prosecution for health and safety violations, even those resulting in death, are often not treated as matter of criminal law per se[1] and may not satisfy public demand that individual organizations be prosecuted and convicted of corporate homicide offences.

The Health and Safety at Work etc. Act 1974 (HSWA) is the primary piece of legislation covering occupational health and safety in the United Kingdom. In the United States at federal level, the current primary piece of legislation governing the regulation of health and safety in the workplace is the Occupational Safety and Health Act 1970 (OSH).[2]

## Health and Safety at Work etc. Act 1974

HSWA was passed to secure the health, safety, and welfare of employees at work and to protect the public from harmful activities of a company's business.[3] The Act set up a national independent regulator for health and

---

[1] P. Almond. 2013. *Corporate Manslaughter and Regulatory Reform* (Basingstoke Hampshire, Palgrave Macmillan) p.22.

[2] The Act was codified in 29 U.S.C. 651 (1970).

[3] HSWA 1974, s1.

safety in the workplace, the Health and Safety Executive (HSE).[4] HSE has multiple functions and duties relating to health and safety in the workplace which include carrying out inspections, reviewing regulations, producing research and statistics, and enforcing the law.[5]

HSWA sets the framework for health and safety regulations in the workplace and is supported by detailed regulations made under it, and non-statutory codes of practice. Some regulations apply across all organizations and other regulations apply to hazards unique to specific industries, such as nuclear or construction.[6]

A core set of regulations known as the "six pack" came into force in 1992[7] (and have since been amended), in order that the United Kingdom could comply with various European directives. These regulations clarify what an employer must do to comply with the requirements of HSWA.

The current regulations are:

- Management of Health and Safety at Work Regulations 1999[8]
- Workplace (Health, Safety and Welfare) Regulations 1992[9]
- Health and Safety (Display Screen Equipment) Regulations 1992[10]
- Personal Protective Equipment at Work Regulations 1992[11]

---

[4] The HSE is a non-departmental public body reporting to the Department for Work and Pensions. It is governed by a Board and the Senior Management Team. The Act originally also set up the Health and Safety Commission whose functions included proposing new laws and standards, conducting research and giving advice on health, safety and welfare in the workplace but this body was merged with the HSE in 2008. http://www.hse.gov.uk/aboutus/40/index.htm (accessed June 6 2017).

[5] HSE may investigate and prosecute breaches of health and safety law but the HSE cannot investigate or prosecute corporate manslaughter or any other criminal offences outside its health and safety remit. http://www.hse.gov.uk/enforce/enforcementguide/wrdeaths/investigation.htm#P2_260 (accessed June 3 2017).

[6] For example, the Construction (Design and Management) Regulations SI2005/51 is the main set of regulations for managing the health, safety and welfare of construction projects.

[7] These have been amended since their first introduction.

[8] SI 1999/3242.

[9] SI 1992/3994.

[10] SI 1992/2792.

[11] SI 1992/2966.

- Manual Handling Operations Regulations 1992[12]
- Provision and Use of Work Equipment Regulations 1998[13]

Most of these regulations are supported by approved codes of practice, produced, or approved by HSE. Employers and others do not have to follow the codes of practice but if prosecuted for breach of any regulations, they will need to prove that their alternative arrangements have the same or better standards of health and safety. The focus of regulatory supervision is risk-assessment-based legislation. The Management of Health and Safety at Work Regulations places a legal duty on employers to carry out a risk assessment and set their own goals in reducing risk. The aim is to reduce the probability of an accident and if an accident does occur, the harmful consequences of it. Other regulations are specifically aimed to prevent death and serious injury.[14] It is a criminal offense to breach a regulation.

## Who Is Covered by HSWA?

The HSWA places general duties and responsibilities on all people at work, including employers, designers, manufacturers, importers and suppliers of goods, occupiers of premises employees, and the self-employed. Liability also extends to members of the public who interfere with safety devices, such as fire escapes.[15]

## Duties Under HSWA

HSWA section 2(1) places a duty on every employer to "ensure, so far as reasonable practical, the health, safety and welfare at work of all his employees." The definition of employee includes trainees and persons on work experience placements.

---

[12]SI 1992/2793.

[13]SI 1998/2306.

[14]For example, the purpose of the Work at Height Regulations SI/2005/732 is to prevent death and injury caused by a fall from height.

[15]HSWA, 1994 s8.

The general duty in section 2(1) is split into more particular duties under section 2(2) which include:

- The provision and maintenance of plant and systems of work[16]
- The use, handling, storage, and transport of articles and substances[17]
- The provision of information, instruction, training, and supervision to ensure the health and safety of employees at work[18]
- The maintenance of any workplace, under the employer's control, in a healthy and safe condition, including any means of access and exit[19]
- The provision and maintenance of a safe and healthy working environment with adequate facilities and arrangements for the welfare of employees at work.[20]

In addition to the duty of the employer to his employees, Section 3 imposes duties on employers to persons who are not their employees[21]:

"It shall be the duty of every employer to conduct his undertaking in such a way to ensure, so far as reasonable practical, that persons not in his employment who may be affected thereby are not thereby exposed to risks to their health and safety."[22]

An "undertaking" means "enterprise" or "business" and an employer/self-employed person retains responsibility for his business even if he sub-contracts it and must take reasonably practicable steps to ensure that a contractor does not expose non-employees to risk.[23] Although liability for a contractor may be excluded where an employer could not have been expected to supervise their activity because the employer did not have the

---

[16]HSWA, 1994 s2 (2) (a).

[17]HSWA, 1994 s2 (2) (b).

[18]HSWA, 1994 s.2 (2) (c).

[19]HSWA, 1994 s.2 (2) (d).

[20]HSWA, 1994 s.2 (2) (e).

[21]92 Members of the public were killed due to work related activities in 2016/17. www.hse.gov.uk/, (accessed June 28 2017).

[22]HSWA, 1994 s3 (1).

[23]*R v. Associated Octel Co Ltd* [1996] 1 WLR 1543.

required specialist knowledge.[24] "Persons not in his employment" ranges from persons working alongside employees, such as independent contractors, to visitors and members of the public.[25]

Self-employed persons have the same duties as employers toward other persons[26] and are also required to protect themselves from risks to their own health and safety if they conduct certain prescribed work.[27] Activities undertaken by the self-employed which are not listed in the Schedule[28] and which do not pose a risk to the health and safety of others are therefore exempted from the scope of HSWA 1974.[29]

HSWA Section 4 imposes a duty on controllers of non-domestic premises to ensure premises are as far as reasonably practicable, safe, and without risks to health. The duty is to persons who are not their employees but who use the premises as a place of work, or use plant and equipment, provided there. Section 6 imposes a duty on a wide range of persons, including designers, manufacturers, importers, and suppliers, in relation to articles or substances provided for use at work. The duty is to ensure that such articles supplied are safe and without risk to health.

HSWA also imposes key liabilities on employees on a personal basis. Section 7 states that an employee is liable for failure to take reasonable care for the safety of others (or himself) and s37 provides that an individual (a director, manager, secretary, or other similar officer) can share criminal liability with the company where the offence has occurred as a result of their consent, connivance, or neglect. Prosecution under Section 7 can be taken against employees at any level in an organization, from the most senior to the most junior employee. Liability under s37 does not require active participation in the commission of the offence and "neglect" can

---

[24] *Haseldine v. CA Daw & Son Ltd* [1941] 2 KB 343. This reflects the civil law position where there is no tortious liability for faults of specialist contractors.

[25] *R v. Tangerine Confectionery Ltd and Veolia ES (UK) Ltd* [2011] EWHC 1137.

[26] HSWA, 1994 s3(2)

[27] These include agriculture, work with asbestos, construction, gas, genetically modified organisms and railway industries.

[28] The Health and Safety at Work etc. Act 1974 (General Duties of Self-Employed Persons) (Prescribed Undertakings) Regulations 2015.

[29] The exemption was introduced by the Deregulation Act 2015.

covers situations where a director should reasonable be expected to be aware that the activities were unsafe.

## Prosecutions Under the Health & Safety at Work Act etc. 1974

Breaches of health and safety legislation provide for both corporate and individual criminal liability. The offences relate to the absence of safety, or a risk to the health and safety of others, and do not require proof of any particular injury. The same offences may be relevant for both fatal and non-fatal injuries. The prosecution have to prove the absence of safety or a risk to health and safety but does not have to show how the accident happened or state what precautions should have been in place.[30] The burden of proof is on the employer to show that it was not reasonably practicable to do more than was done to comply with the duty.

In 2015/16, 144 workers were killed in the work place. This represents 0.46 per 100,000 full-time equivalent workers.[31]

HSE (or another relevant enforcing authority) investigates and, where appropriate, prosecute breaches of health and safety law. If, during

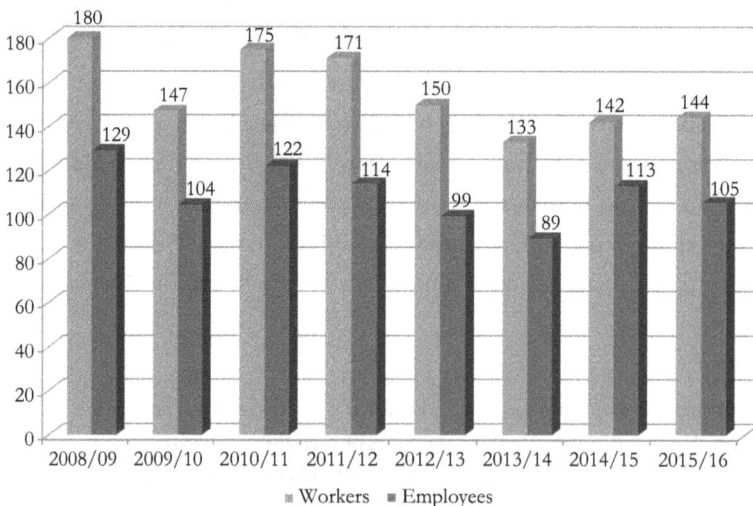

Chart 3.1 U.K. fatalities of workers in the workplace 2008–2016.[32]

---

[30]R v. Chargot [2008] UKHL 73.

[31]www.hse.gov.uk/statistics/pdf/fatalinjuries.pdf, (accessed June 28 2017).

[32]http://www.hse.gov.uk/statistics/, (accessed June 28 2017).

the course of their investigation, evidence is found suggesting corporate manslaughter, the case is passed to the police to investigate.[33] Where there is a charge of corporate manslaughter, there may also be a charge against the same defendant, in the same proceedings, for a health and safety offence, arising out of some or all of those circumstances. The majority of cases following a fatality involved breaches by employers of section 2 or 3 HSWA.[34]

## Occupational Safety and Health Act 1970

OSH aims to ensure worker and workplace safety and health by imposing comprehensive duties on employers and severe penalties in the event of a breach. OSH created the Occupational Safety and Health Administration[35] (OSHA), which has similar enforcement functions as the HSE. OSHA sets and enforces protective workplace safety and health standards, carries out inspections and provides information, education, training, and assistance to employers and workers. OSH also set up the National Institute for Occupational Safety and Health (NIOSH)[36] as a research agency on safety and health in workplaces.

OSH permits individual states to set up their own safety and health standards and enforcement, provided the plans are "at least as effective in providing safe and healthful employment and places of employment as the standards promulgated" under OSHA.[37] To date, 26 states and 2 U.S. territories operate state plans.[38] The majority of state plans adopt federal

---

[33]HSE. 2015. Enforcement Policy Statement. http://www.hse.gov.uk/enforce/enforcementguide/wrdeaths/investigation.htm, (accessed June 13 2017).

[34]http://www.hse.gov.uk/prosecutions/case/case_list.asp?PN=2&ST=C&EO=%3D&SN=F&x=19&SF=FAT&SV=Yes&y=17&SO=DODS, (accessed June 28 2017).

[35]OSHA is part of the United States Department of Labor. https://www.osha.gov/about.html, (accessed June 13 2017).

[36]NIOSH is part of the U.S. federal government's Centers for Disease Control and Prevention. For further information on NIOSH see their website at https://www.cdc.gov/niosh/about/default.html, (accessed June 26 2017.

[37] OSH 1970, s18.

[38]Arizona, California, Hawaii, Indiana, Iowa, Kentucky, Maryland, Michigan, Minnesota, Nevada, New Mexico, North Carolina, Oregon, South Carolina, Tennessee,

standards verbatim although some states, such as California, have chosen to adopt stricter standards.[39]

## Who Is Covered by OSH?

Most private sector employers and their employees in the 50 states, the District of Columbia, Puerto Rico, and other U.S. territories are covered by OSH. Coverage is provided either directly by the Federal OSHA or by an OSHA-approved state plan. Federal agencies must have a safety and health program that meets the same standards as private employers.[40] Employees who work for state and local governments are not covered unless they work in states that have an OSHA-approved state plan.[41] The Act does not cover, self-employed persons, farms which employ only immediate members of the farmer's family and workplace hazards regulated by another federal agency (for example, the Mine Safety and Health Administration, the Department of Energy, or Coast Guard).[42]

In 2015, 4836 workers in the United States were killed in the work place. This represents 3.4 per 100,000 full-time equivalent workers.[43]

---

Utah, Vermont, Virginia, Washington, Wyoming, and Puerto Rico, have state OSHA approved plans that cover both private and state and local government workplaces. Connecticut, Illinois, Maine, New Jersey, New York, and Virgin Islands, have state OSHA approved-plans that cover public sector workers only. https://www.osha.gov/dcsp/osp/, (accessed May 21 2017).

[39]http://safety.blr.com/workplace-safety-news/safety-administration/OSHA-Occupational-Safety-and-Health-Administration/Federal-vs.-state-OSHA-Do-you-understand-the-diffe/, (accessed June 22 2017).

[40]https://www.osha.gov/workers/index.html, (accessed June 22 2017).

[41]Some states have plans that only cover public sector workers. See fn38 above.

[42]Occupational Safety and Health Administration. 2016. Workers' Rights, OSHA 3021-11R 2016 p.5.

[43]https://www.osha.gov/oshstats/commonstats.html (accessed 3 June 2017).

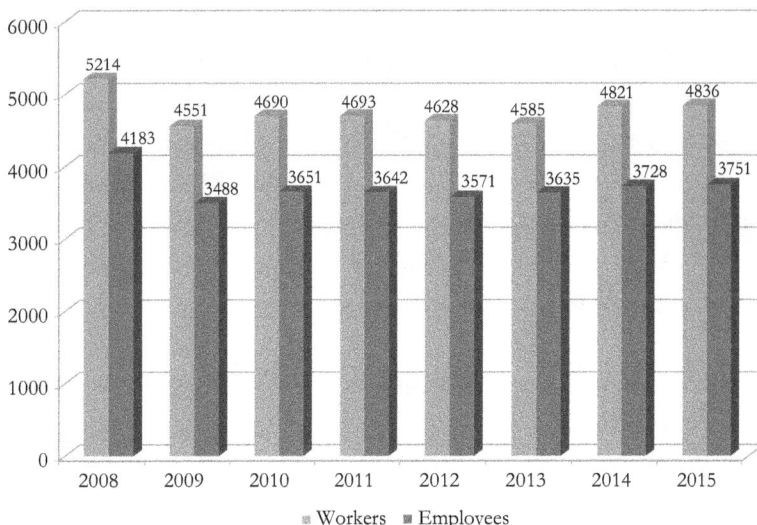

**Chart 3.2  U.S. fatalities of workers in the workplace 2008–2015.**[44]

# Duties Under the OSH

There is a general duty clause in OSH which requires employers to provide their employees with a place of employment that "is free from recognizable hazards that are causing or likely to cause death or serious harm to employees."[45]

This clause has been interpreted by the courts to mean that an employer has a legal obligation to provide a workplace free of conditions or activities that either the employer or industry recognizes as hazardous (this includes hazards that are obvious, and ones that the employer knew or should have known about, and hazards recognized within the relevant industry). The conditions or activities must cause, or be likely to cause, death or serious physical harm to employees and there must be a feasible method of correcting the hazard.[46]

---

[44]https://www.osha.gov/oshstats/index.html, (accessed June 3 2017).

[45]OSH s5(a)(1),

[46] https://www.osha.gov/SLTC/workplaceviolence/standards.html, (accessed June 22 2017).

In addition, OSH provides that each employer "shall comply with occupational safety and health standards promulgated under this Act."[47] OSHA standards are rules that describe the methods that employers must use to protect their employees from hazards. These standards also limit the amount of hazardous chemicals, substances, or noise that workers can be exposed to and require the use of certain safe work practices and equipment.[48]

OSHA sets four groups of standards designed to protect workers from a wide range of hazards:

- General industry (which applies to the largest group of workers and worksites)
- Construction
- Maritime
- Agriculture

The general duty clause can be used to regulate hazards where OSHA has not provided specific standards. Employees must also comply with all OSHA requirements that apply to their actions and conduct.[49]

## Prosecutions Under OSH

OSH states that criminal penalties may be imposed on any employer who willfully violates a safety standard, rule or order pursuant to OSH Act, where that violation causes the death of any employee.[50] Four elements must be proved by the prosecution in order to establish a criminal liability. These are:

- The defendant is an employer engaged in a business affecting commerce

---

[47]OSH 1970, s5(a)(2).
[48]Occupational Safety and Health Administration. 2016. Workers' Rights, 3021-11R p.7 https://www.osha.gov/Publications/osha3021.pdf, (accessed June 22 2017).
[49]OSH 1970, s5(b).
[50]OSH 1970, s17.

- The employer violated a "standard, rule or order" promulgated pursuant to 29 U.S.C. 665, or any regulation prescribed under OSH
- The violation was willful
- The violation caused the death of an employee.

"Engaged in a business affecting commerce" is interpreted broadly[51] and includes employers who are not engaged in interstate business. "Employer" also includes an individual who is a corporate officer or a director.[52] Although if not charged as principal, a corporate officer or director cannot be charged as aiding and abetting. "Willful" means if it is "done knowingly and purposely by an employer who, having a free will or choice, either intentionally disregards the standard or is plainly indifferent to its requirement. An omission or failure to act is willfully done if committed voluntarily and intentionally."[53]

The prosecution must prove beyond reasonable doubt that the conduct or omission, which amounts to the violation of the OSHA standard, was both the factual cause and the "legal cause" (i.e., the harm was a foreseeable and natural result of the conduct) of the injury resulting in the fatality. Where it can be shown that there has been intentional disregard or plain indifference to the requirements of the law, ignorance of an applicable standard is not a defense.[54]

---

[51] *Usery v. Lacy (Aqua View Apartments)*, 628 F.2d 1226 (9th Cir. 1980).

[52] *United States v. Doig*, 950 F.2d 411, 415 (7th Cir. 1991).

[53] *United States v. Dye Construction Co.*, 510 F.2d 78 (10th Cir. 1975).

[54] *Georgia Electric Co. v. Marshall*, 595 F.2d 309 (5th Cir 1979).

# CHAPTER 4

# Penalties

The penalties for convicted offenders in the United Kingdom are set out in CMCHA. The offense of corporate manslaughter is punishable by way of a fine. The Act also creates two other penalties that may be imposed by the sentencing judge in addition to the fine, namely a remedial order (s9) and a publicity order (s10).

A court has to take into account the guidelines issued by the Sentencing Council (formerly known as the Sentencing Guidelines Council)[1] – an independent body composed of judicial and nonjudicial members, chaired by the Lord Chief Justice – when determining the final penalty. The guidelines and CMCHA work in tandem.

The initial sentencing guidelines for corporations convicted of corporate manslaughter were published in 2010.[2] These were subsequently amended pursuant to an extensive review of sentencing under CMCHA, and the amended guidelines published in 2015[3] (effective in any case sentenced on or after February 1, 2016 regardless of the date of the offense).

## Sentence by Way of Fine

The offense of corporate manslaughter is indictable only and on conviction the judge may impose an unlimited fine (section 1(6)).

---

[1]Under the provisions of section 125 (1) of the Coroners and Justice Act 2009 the guidelines must be taken into account by the courts when passing a sentence.

[2]Sentencing Guidelines Council. 2010. *Corporate Manslaughter & Health and Safety Offences Causing Death: Definitive Guideline.* https://www.sentencingcouncil.org.uk/publications/item/corporate-manslaughter-health-and-safety-offenses-causing-death-definitive-guideline/(accessed May 25 2017).

[3]Sentencing Council. 2015. *Health and Safety Offences, Corporate Manslaughter and Food Safety and Hygiene Offences: Definitive Guideline.* https://www.sentencingcouncil.org.uk/wp-content/uploads/HS-offenses-definitive-guideline-FINAL-web.pdf (accessed May 5 2017).

There will inevitably be a broad range of fines because of the range of seriousness involved and the differences in the circumstances of the defendants. The fine is designed to punish the corporate defendant and is therefore tailored not only to what the corporation has done but also to its individual circumstances.

When setting the fine, the court has to refer to the sentencing guidelines. According to these, fines must be punitive and sufficient to have an impact on the defendant.

The guidelines specify a number of categories for the calculation by the courts of the financial penalty. These are determined by reference to the size of the corporate defendant; size being calculated on the basis of turnover. For the purposes of sentencing, a micro company has a turnover of no more than £2m; a small company has a turnover of between £2m and £10m; a medium company a turnover of between £10m and £50m; and a large company a turnover in excess of £50m.

Within each category are two sentencing ranges and "starting points" which define the position within the ranges from which to start calculating the sentence. In order to determine which range is appropriate for any given offender, the sentencing judge has to consider the degree of culpability of the offender and the harm caused – in other words, whether it is an offense of higher (A) or lower (B) culpability.

For example, for the smallest, "micro," organizations (turnover of up to £2 million) convicted of an offense of lower culpability (B) the

*Table 4.1 Penalties for corporate manslaughter*

| Size of organization | Starting point | Category range |
|---|---|---|
| Large:<br>Turnover more than £50 million | £7,500,000 (A: more serious offences)<br>£5,000,000 (B) | £4,800,000–£20,000,000<br>£3,000,000–£12,500,000 |
| Medium:<br>Turnover £10 million to £50 million | £3,000,000 (A: more serious offences)<br>£2,000,000 (B) | £1,800,000–£7,500,000<br>£1,200,000–£5,000,000 |
| Small:<br>Turnover £2 million to £10 million | £800,000 (A: more serious offences)<br>£540,000 (B) | £540,000–£2,800,000<br>£350,000–£2,000,000 |
| Micro:<br>Turnover up to £2 million | £450,000 (A: more serious offences)<br>£300,000 (B) | £270,000–£800,000<br>£180,000–£540,000 |

starting point is £300,000, with the range commencing at £180,000. At the upper end of the scale, where the offenders are large companies (£50+ million turnover) and the offense one of the gravest forms (A) (for example, where there has been cost cutting at the expense of safety and a poor record of health and safety), the starting point is £7.5m and the range, £4.8m – £20m.

## Assessing Culpability

The 2015 guidelines provide that culpability should be assessed by considering four questions:

1. How foreseeable was serious injury?
   The more foreseeable a serious injury was, the graver the offense. Failure to respond appropriately to "near misses" arising in similar circumstances may be factors indicating greater foreseeability of injury.
2. How far short of the applicable standard did the defendant fall?
   Lack of adherence to recognized standards in the industry or the inadequacy of training, supervision, and reporting arrangements would be relevant factors for consideration by a sentencing judge.
3. How common is this kind of breach in this organization?
   Where the noncompliance was widespread and systemic, the level of culpability is likely to be high.
4. Was there more than one death, or a high risk of further deaths, or serious personal injury in addition to death?
   The greater the number of deaths or very serious personal injuries, the greater the level of culpability.

The guidelines also provide a non-exhaustive list of factual circumstances which would aggravate or mitigate the offense:

## Aggravating Factors

- Previous convictions, having regard to (a) the nature of the offense to which the conviction relates and its relevance to the current offense; and (b) the time that has elapsed since the conviction;

- Cost-cutting at the expense of safety;
- Deliberate concealment of illegal nature of activity;
- Breach of any court order;
- Obstruction of justice;
- Poor health and safety record;
- Falsification of documentation or licenses;
- Deliberate failure to obtain or comply with relevant licenses in order to avoid scrutiny by authorities;
- Offender exploited vulnerable victims.

## Factors Reducing Seriousness or Reflecting Mitigation

- No previous convictions or no relevant/recent convictions;
- Evidence of steps taken to remedy problem;
- High level of co-operation with the investigation, beyond that which will always be expected;
- Good health and safety record;
- Effective health and safety procedures in place;
- Self-reporting, co-operation and acceptance of responsibility;
- Other events beyond the responsibility of the offender contributed to the death (however, actions of victims are unlikely to be considered contributory events). Offenders are required to protect workers or others who are neglectful of their own safety in a way which is reasonably foreseeable.

Courts then identify whether any combination of these, or other relevant factors, should result in an upward or downward adjustment from the starting point.

Since CMCHA entered the statute book in 2007, there have been 25 convictions (see table 4:2 below), with fines ranging from £8,000 to £1,200,000, and five acquittals.[4]

The guidelines also set out the fiscal procedure for the calculation of penalties. Comprehensive accounts for the previous three years have to be made available to the court by the convicted organization, in order that

---

[4]www.cps.gov.uk (accessed June 30 2017); http://www.hse.gov.uk/Prosecutions/ (accessed June 30 2017).

*Table 4.2  Convictions under CMCHA, April 2008 to May 2017*

| Year | Defendant company | Plea/Trial | Fine |
|------|-------------------|------------|------|
| 2011 | Cotswold Geotechnical (Holdings) Ltd | Trial | £385,000 |
| 2012 | JMW Farm Ltd | Guilty Plea | £187,500 |
| 2012 | Lion Steel Ltd | Guilty Plea | £480,000 |
| 2013 | J Murray & Sons Ltd | Guilty Plea | £100,000 |
| 2013 | Princes' Sporting Club Ltd | Guilty Plea | £134,579 |
| 2014 | Mobile Sweepers (Reading) Ltd | Guilty Plea | £8,000 |
| 2014 | Cavendish Masonry Ltd | Trial | £150,000 |
| 2014 | Sterecycle (Rotherham) Ltd | Trial | £500,000 |
| 2014 | A. Diamond & Son (Timber) Ltd | Guilty Plea | £75,000 |
| 2014 | DIECI Ltd & Nicole Enterprise Ltd | Guilty Plea | £100,000 |
| 2015 | Peter Mawson Ltd | Guilty Plea | £200,000 |
| 2015 | Pyranha Mouldings Ltd | Trial | £200,000 |
| 2015 | Baldwins Crane Hire Ltd | Trial | £700,000 |
| 2015 | CAV Aerospace Ltd | Trial | £1,000,000 |
| 2015 | Huntley Mount Engineering Ltd | Guilty Plea | £150,000 |
| 2015 | Kings Scaffolding Ltd | Trial | £300,000 |
| 2015 | Cheshire Gate and Automation Ltd | Guilty Plea | £50,000 |
| 2015 | Linley Developments Ltd | Guilty Plea | £225,000 |
| 2016 | Sherwood Rise Ltd | Guilty Plea | £30,000 |
| 2016 | Bilston Skips Ltd | Trial | £600,000 |
| 2016 | Monavon Construction Ltd | Guilty Plea | £550,000 |
| 2017 | SR and RJ Brown Ltd | Guilty Plea | £300,000 |
| 2017 | Martinisation (London) Ltd | Trial | £1,200,000 |
| 2017 | Koseoglu Metalworks Ltd | Trial | £300,000 |
| 2017 | Ozdil Investments Ltd | Trial | £500,000 |

its financial status be accurately assessed. In addition, when quantifying the level of the fine courts have to take into consideration: turnover; profit before tax; directors' remuneration, loan accounts, and pension provision; and assets as disclosed by the balance sheet. Should a court not be satisfied that sufficient reliable information has been provided it may infer that the offender can afford to pay any penalty.

Notwithstanding the sentencing mechanism proposed, there is also discretion for the courts to move outside the suggested ranges in order to achieve a proportionate sentence.

The cost of fines cannot be met by insurance. Such risks are deemed to be uninsurable at law. For public policy reasons, any insurance contract purporting to insure against the risk of criminal fines would be void and unenforceable. It is recognized that if a fine imposed on company is substantial, the result may be its demise.

## Remedial and Publicity Orders

Under s9, an organization can be ordered to take steps to remedy the management failure that led to the death. Remedial Orders are available in cases where corporate failings have not been remedied by the time of the trial, and where such failings are "sufficiently specific to be enforceable."[5] Failure to comply with the order is punishable on conviction by an unlimited fine. The power under s9 is very similar to the power afforded to a judge under HWSA s42. These powers have rarely, if ever, been exercised.

Under s10, a court can impose a publicity order in addition to the fine.[6] This in effect is a "naming and shaming" of convicted corporations – requiring the organization to publicize its conviction, details of the particulars of the offense, the amount of any fine and the terms of any remedial order that has been imposed. Failure to comply with the order is also punishable on conviction by an unlimited fine.

Princes Sporting Club Limited was the first company to be issued with a publicity order under s10. In 2013, the Sporting Club had pleaded guilty following the death of an 11-year-old girl during a water sports activity.[7] The purpose of the publicity order was to act as a warning to

---

[5]Sentencing Guidelines Council. 2010. *Corporate Manslaughter & Health and Safety Offences Causing Death: Definitive Guideline* para 35.https://www.sentencingcouncil.org.uk/publications/item/corporate-manslaughter-health-and-safety-offences-causing-death-definitive-guideline/(accessed May 5 2017).
[6]CMCHA 2007, s10.
[7]This is the only case to date where a company has been convicted of the corporate manslaughter of a member of the public rather than a worker and also the first such case relating to a company no longer trading. Princes Sporting Club Limited had ceased trading in November 2012. The accounts for the year ending March 31, s2013 show a net book value of £693,604 and net liabilities of £970,912. The parent

other operators (it would not have an impact on the company itself since it had ceased trading before the trial).

Publicity orders have since been imposed on other corporate offenders, although they still remain rare.[8] In 2015 upon conviction of Peter Mawson Ltd following the death of an employee who had fallen through a skylight onto concrete, the court ordered the company to advertise the facts of its conviction through a half-page advertisement in a local newspaper and a notice on its own website.[9]

Critics however question the efficacy of such orders on small firms since in relation to small companies there may be little or no significant reputation to be lost through stigmatic punishment.[10]

## Penalties for Breaches of Health & Safety Legislation

### Health and Safety at Work etc Act (HSWA) 1974

Companies that face manslaughter charges are also usually prosecuted in respect of breaches of regulatory provisions under the Health and Safety at Work etc Act (HSWA) 1974. Many cases in fact contain multiple counts on the indictment. Although there are overlaps between corporate manslaughter and health and safety offenses, the offenses are different. Crucially, HSWA makes no distinction between fatal and non-fatal incidents. In addition, while individuals cannot be liable under CMCHA (although remain vulnerable to prosecution for the common law offense of gross negligence manslaughter), breaches of health and safety legislation specifically provide for both corporate and individual criminal liability.

Offenses under HSWA are triable either way, i.e., in the Magistrates' Court or Crown Court, depending on the seriousness of the alleged offense.

---

company, Princes Water Ski Club, made a loss of £118,779 with net assets of £776,458 on 31 March 2013. H. Fidderman. 2014. "Fifth corporate manslaughter case claims first non-worker." *Health and Safety Bulletin* 426:15.

[8]See for example, Mobile Sweepers Reading Ltd; Peter Mawson Ltd; Linley Developments Ltd.

[9]N. Barrett. 2015. "News in Brief" 26(2) *Construction Law* 5(1); see also *http://www.endole.co.uk/company/04330564/peter-mawson-limited* (accessed August 21 2015).

[10]V.S. Khanna. 1996. "Corporate Criminal Liability: What Purpose Does it Serve?" *Harvard Law Review* 109, pp. 1477-1534.

The sanctions available for breaches of HWSA are:

A) An unlimited fine;
B) A remedial order.

HSWA s42 provides that the court can impose a remedial order in instead of or in addition to any other sentence. Failure to comply with the remedial order is an offense punishable on indictment by an unlimited fine (and/or a maximum two years imprisonment for an individual);

C) A custodial sentence.

In addition to or as an alternative to a fine, an individual can face a term of imprisonment of up to 12 months on conviction for most offenses under HSWA 1974 in the Magistrates Court and up to two years on conviction in the Crown Court. Following a guilty plea to the charge of corporate manslaughter, for example, Peter Mawson Ltd was fined £220,000 (as well as costs of £31,500). Alongside his company, its proprietor (Peter Mawson) also pleaded guilty to associated health and safety charges and was sentenced to eight months in prison (suspended for two years) and required to carry out 200 hours of unpaid work.[11]

The court has no power to make a publicity order as it does under CMCHA; however, the Health and Safety Executive has published details of organizations convicted of health and safety offenses since 2000.

In the United States, the primary piece of federal legislation governing the regulation of health and safety in the work place is the Occupational Safety and Health (OSH) Act 1970. Like HSWA 1974, OSH is intended to provide legal protection to workers by imposing comprehensive duties on employers and severe penalties in the event of a breach. The Occupational Health and Safety Administration (OSHA) established under OSH imposes mandatory standards, compliance guidance and penalties, both civil and criminal.

Section 17 OSH sets out the penalties that can be imposed on an employer in breach of their obligations under, or deriving from, the Act. For

---

[11]http://www.bbc.co.uk/news/uk-england-cumbria-31120968(accessed July 7 2017).

each breach, the civil penalty is a fine of $7,000. Under the original OSH provisions, where death of an employee occurred and there had been a "willful or repeated" breach of an OSH standard, the level of the fine increased substantially, to between $5,000 and $70,000. However, these provisions have since been amended: Where death of an employee occurs and there has been willful breach of an OSH standard, there is provision under 29 U.S.C. ss666 (e) 2000 for referral to the Department of Justice for criminal prosecution. Willful violation of OSH is now classified as a criminal "Class B misdemeanor" and conviction in such a case carries a maximum custodial sentence of six months and a fine of up to $250,000 for an individual and $500,000 for a corporate defendant. Historically, these provisions have been used sparingly[12] and as a result, states have instead tended to opt for prosecutions for work-related deaths via general homicide legislation, and at the state level. Nonetheless, recent indications are that there is greater willingness on the part of federal prosecutors to pursue willful violations of health and safety regulations.[13]

In the United Kingdom, HSWA is enforced by the Health and Safety Executive (HSE) rather than criminal justice agencies. The HSE tends to adopt a compliance strategy and prefers advice and assistance to companies over prosecution. Nonetheless, where there has been a fatality, there will normally be an investigation by the HSE, and in the event of a breach of health and safety regulations leading to a fatality, a prosecution.[14]

### Health & Safety (Offences) Act 2008 (HSOA)

The spectrum of health and safety offenses falling under HSWA 1974 tend to be seen as regulatory or quasi crime, but the advent of the Health and Safety (Offences) Act (HSOA) 2008 has given much greater bite to what is an important part of the criminal law by increasing the severity of sentences.

---

[12]In 2008, it was calculated that there had been a mere 68 prosecutions in the 28 years that the statute had been in force: L. Rhinehart. 2008. "The Unfulfilled Promise of the Occupational Safety and Health Act." 111 *West Virginia Law Review* 117, at p124.

[13]www.osha.gov/newsrelease.html (accessed June 29 2017).

[14]http://www.hse.gov.uk/Prosecutions/ (accessed June 30 2017).

HSOA came into force in the United Kingdom on 16 January 2009 and applies to offenses committed from that date. The 2008 Act does not create new offenses but scales up the maximum financial penalties available in the lower courts for breaches of HSWA 1974 and health and safety regulations, and makes terms of imprisonment a penalty for additional health and safety offenses. The maximum fine which may be imposed in the Magistrates Court for most health and safety offenses is now £20,000. The power of the Crown Court to impose unlimited fines is unaltered.

The real effect of HSOA is likely to be in respect of individual defendants, both employers and company directors, who could be facing terms of imprisonment for a greater number of offenses and longer terms for the most serious offenses. However, the Act makes little difference to corporate defendants where in the most serious cases unlimited fines already existed under HSWA.

# Bibliography

## Books

P. Almond 2013. *Corporate Manslaughter and Regulatory Reform* (Basingstoke, Hampshire: Palgrave Macmillan).

J. C. Coffee. 1983. "Corporate Criminal Responsibility," in S. Kadish (ed). *Encyclopaedia of Crime and Justice* (New York: Free Press), pp253-264.

J.C. Coffee. 1999. "Corporate Criminal Liability: An Introduction and Comparative Survey," in A. Eser et al. (eds). *Criminal Responsibility of Legal and Collective Entities* (Berlin: Edition Iuscrim), pp9-38.

G. Forlin 2014. *Corporate Liability: Work Related Deaths and Criminal Prosecutions* (London: Bloomsbury).

A. Pinto & M. Evans. 2008. *Corporate Criminal Liability* (London: Sweet & Maxwell).

C. Wells. 2001. *Corporations, Crime and Accountability,* 2nd ed. (Oxford: OUP).

## Journal articles

N. Barrett. 2015. "News in Brief" 26(2) *Construction Law* 5(1).

H. Fidderman. 2014. "Fifth Corporate Manslaughter Case Claims First Non-worker," *Health and Safety Bulletin* 426,15.

J. W. Harlow. 2011. "Corporate Criminal Liability for Homicide: A Statutory Framework," *Duke Law Journal* 61(1) p123.

V.S. Khanna. 1996. "Corporate Criminal Liability: What Purpose Does it Serve?" *Harvard Law Review* 109, pp1477-1534.

L. Rhinehart. 2008. "The Unfulfilled Promise of the Occupational Safety and Health Act." 111 *West Virginia Law Review* 117.

## Legislation

### U.K. Statutes

Coroners and Justice Act 2009.

Corporate Manslaughter and Corporate Homicide Act 2007.

The Deregulation Act 2015.

Health and Safety at Work etc. Act 1974.
Health & Safety (Offences) Act 2008.
Human Rights Act 1998.

## U.K. Statutory Instruments

Construction (Design and Management) Regulations SI2005/51.
The Corporate Manslaughter and Corporate Homicide Act 2007 (Commencement No. 1) Order 2008 SI 2008/401.
The Corporate Manslaughter and Corporate Homicide Act 2007 (Commencement No. 3) Order 2011 SI 2011/1867.
Health and Safety (Display Screen Equipment) Regulations SI/1992/2792.
The Health and Safety at Work etc. Act 1974 (General Duties of Self-Employed Persons) (Prescribed Undertakings) Regulations 2015 SI2015/1585.
Management of Health and Safety at Work Regulations SI 1999/3242.
Manual Handling Operations Regulations SI/1992/2793.
Personal Protective Equipment at Work Regulations SI/1992/2966.
Provision and Use of Work Equipment Regulations SI1998/2306.
Work at Height Regulations SI/2005/732.
Workplace (Health, Safety and Welfare) Regulations SI 1992/3994.

## U.S. Statutes

The Occupational Safety and Health Act 1970.

## Cases

### U.K. Cases

*Coppen v. Moore (No 2)* [1898] 2 QB 306 (DC).
*Haseldine v. CA Daw & Son Ltd* [1941] 2 KB 343.
*Haughton v. Smith* [1975] AC 476.
*R v. Adomako* [1994] 3 WLR 288.
*R v. Associated Octel Co Ltd* [1996] 1 WLR 1543.
*R v. Bateman* (1925) 19 Cr App R 8.
*R v. Chargot* [2008] UKHL 73.
*R v. Great North of England Railway Company* (1846) 9 QB 315 (DC).
*R v. HM Coroner for East Kent ex p Spooner* (1989) 88 Cr App R 10 (DC).
*R v. Kite* [1996] 2 Cr. App. R. (S) 295.

*R v. Miller* [1983] *1 All ER 978.*

*R v. P&O Ferries (Dover) Ltd* (1990) 93 Cr App R 72.

*R v. Tangerine Confectionery Limited and Veolia ES (UK) Limited* [2011] EWHC 1137.


## U.S. Cases

*Georgia Electric Co. v. Marshall*, 595 F.2d 309 (5th Cir.1979).

*New York Central and Hudson River Railroad Company v. United States* (1909) 212 U.S. 481.

*People of the State of New York v. Ebasco Services Incorporated*, 77 Misc.2d 784 (1974).

*People v. Rochester Railway and Light Co.* (1909) 195 NY 102.

*United States v. Doig*, 950 F.2d 411, 415 (7th Cir. 1991).

*United States v. Dye Construction Co.*, 510 F.2d 78 (10th Cir. 1975).

*Usery v. Lacy (Aqua View Apartments)*, 628 F.2d 1226 (9th Cir. 1980).

*U.S. v. Time-DC*, 381 F Supp 730 (WD Pa, 1974).

*U.S. v. Bank of New England, 821 F 2d 844 (1st Circuit).*


## U.K. government reports, guides and policy statements

HSE. 2015. Enforcement Policy Statement. http://www.hse.gov.uk/enforce/enforcepolicy.htm

Ministry of Justice. 2007. *Guide to the Corporate Manslaughter and Corporate Homicide Act 2007.* https://www.justice.gov.uk/downloads/legislation/bills-acts/circulars/moj/corporate-manslaughter-act-2007-circular-9-feb-08.pdf

Occupational Safety and Health Administration. 2016. *Workers' Rights.* 2016. 3021-11R. https://www.osha.gov/Publications/osha3021.pdf

Sentencing Council. 2015. *Health and Safety Offences, Corporate Manslaughter and Food Safety and Hygiene Offences: Definitive Guideline.* https://www.sentencingcouncil.org.uk/wp-content/uploads/HS-offenses-definitive-guideline-FINAL-web.pdf

Sentencing Guidelines Council. 2010. *Corporate Manslaughter & Health and Safety Offences Causing Death: Definitive Guideline.* https://www.sentencingcouncil.org.uk/publications/item/corporate-manslaughter-health-and-safety-offenses-causing-death-definitive-guideline/

U.K. Parliamentary Defence Select Committee. 2016. *Beyond Endurance? Military exercises and the Duty of Care.* HC598. https://www.publications.parliament.uk/pa/cm201516/cmselect/cmdfence/598/598.pdf

## Websites

http://www.hse.gov.uk/
https://www.osha.gov/
www.osha.gov/newsrelease.html
https://www.cdc.gov/niosh/
http://www.cps.gov.uk/
https://www.healthandsafetyatwork.com/
http://www.tetraconsulting.co.uk/
http://www.theguardian.com/uk
http://www.parliament.uk/
http://www.hse.gov.uk/Prosecutions/
http://www.bbc.co.uk/news/uk-england-cumbria-31120968

# Index

# OTHER TITLES IN OUR BUSINESS LAW COLLECTION

John Wood, Econautics Sustainability Institute, *Editor*

- *Preventing Litigation: An Early Warning System to Get Big Value out of Big Data* by Nelson E. Brestoff and William H. Inmon
- *Understanding Consumer Bankruptcy: A Guide for Businesses, Managers, and Creditors* by Scott B. Kuperberg
- *The History of Economic Thought: A Concise Treatise for Business, Law, and Public Policy, Volume I: From the Ancients Through Keynes* by Robert Ashford and Stefan Padfield
- *Buyer Beware: The Hidden Cost of Labor in an International Merger and Acquisition* by Elvira Medici and Linda J. Spievack
- *The History of Economic Thought: A Concise Treatise for Business, Law, and Public Policy, Volume II: After Keynes, Through the Great Recession and Beyond* by Robert Ashford and Stefan Padfield
- *European Employment Law: A Brief Guide to the Essential Elements* by Claire-Michelle Smyth

Business Expert Press has over 30 collection in business subjects such as finance, marketing strategy, sustainability, public relations, economics, accounting, corporate communications, and many others. For more information about all our collections, please visit www.businessexpertpress.com/collections.

Business Expert Press is actively seeking collection editors as well as authors. For more information about becoming an BEP author or collection editor, please visit http://www.businessexpertpress.com/author

# Announcing the Business Expert Press Digital Library

*Concise e-books business students need for classroom and research*

This book can also be purchased in an e-book collection by your library as

- a one-time purchase,
- that is owned forever,
- allows for simultaneous readers,
- has no restrictions on printing, and
- can be downloaded as PDFs from within the library community.

Our digital library collections are a great solution to beat the rising cost of textbooks. E-books can be loaded into their course management systems or onto students' e-book readers. The **Business Expert Press** digital libraries are very affordable, with no obligation to buy in future years. For more information, please visit **www.businessexpertpress.com/librarians**. To set up a trial in the United States, please email **sales@businessexpertpress.com**.

www.ingramcontent.com/pod-product-compliance
Lightning Source LLC
Chambersburg PA
CBHW071123210326
41519CB00020B/6398